Local Habitation

By Peter Dale

Peter Dale
Local Habitation

A Sequence of Poems

ANVIL PRESS POETRY

Published in 2009
by Anvil Press Poetry Ltd
Neptune House 70 Royal Hill London SE10 8RF
www.anvilpresspoetry.com

ISBN 978 0 85646 418 8

This book is published
with financial assistance from
Arts Council England

A catalogue record for this book
is available from the British Library

Designed and set in Monotype Ehrhardt by Anvil
Printed and bound in England
by Cromwell Press Group
Trowbridge, Wiltshire

ACKNOWLEDGEMENTS

Versions of some of these poems have appeared in the
following publications: *Acumen*; *Agenda*; *Dream Catcher*;
Meridian; *Outposts*; *Quattrocento*; *The Rialto*;
The Swansea Review.

'Lead', 'Oriel' and 'Soliloquy' were first published in
Peter Dale in Conversation with Cynthia Haven,
Between the Lines Press, 2005.

IN MEMORIAM

Keith D. Dale 1942–1995
Elizabeth L. Dale 1965–1965
Simon Dale 1967–1967

Let me not to the marriage of true minds
Admit impediments.

SHAKESPEARE, Sonnet 116

No one in their right mind loses
their secret anonymity.

JOANNA LUMLEY,
interviewed in *The Radio Times*

Contents

III

IV

V

Note

ON THE narrative level, this sequence concerns Dan's first love with a feisty, earth-earthy woman, Gill. The affair ends abruptly. Dan encounters and marries another, Jo. Life moves on to the joy of birth, the mourning for the infant's death, its aftermath in the development of the relationship and life's passing on and away.

On the subjective level, it deals with the voices of these protagonists, rooted in local habitations, weaving in and out of the speech and consciousness of each of them with all the tones, nuances, poignancies, pleasures and regrets of hindsight with its shifts in recollection, the voluntary and involuntary self-editing of memory and mismemory. There is a ghostly eternal triangle whose angles are ruled feint or bold in response to situation, time and change.

The characters' speech, thoughts, memories and mismemories are differentiated in the text by the following methods. The names of characters involved in each poem are printed under the title. The space allotted between the names indicates the indent within the poem that marks the person speaking, being cited, remembered, or misremembered. The man's text is always set to the left; there are two levels of indented text for the two women.

When a name under a title is in brackets it indicates that some sort of remembrance, rather than speech, is happening in that poem. Poems in the form of dialogue always have speech marks.

I

Draw

Dan   Gill

    'You're like a fly circling the centre light,
    ceaselessly. Stop it.'
'I'll make a deal with you:
get out of my mind, get out of my sight
and Monday fortnight, say, haunt me in lieu:
yowl and wail or try your banshee screech.
You traverse skulls without a bit of plaster
so waltz through walls with your infrangible breach.
Articulate the coming of disaster.

'You'll not craze me with any see-through stuff.
I'll lay you before the crowing of the cock –
revenant, spectre, wraith, in chains or buff.
Wall-perviants can't purport much interference.'
    'If walls could rearrange my due appearance,
    I might come then – with something of a shock.'

Duologue

Dan   Gill

'Dearest, you're trembling to my touch
because your flesh is birds
that any shadowing perturbs
and these mere words will flush.'

> 'Some hopes. I'm trembling to this stroke
> of yours because I saw at dawn
> my hand outside the blankets form
> a turkey's head and throat.'

Continuo

(Dan) Gill

> 'You cannot lure me,
> spell-proof my person.
> You will not lay me.
>
> 'Let's hear you play me
> your full diapason.
> Try that to lure me.
>
> 'First, hullabaloo me
> and call it passion.
> That will not lay me.

'Next, speak sublimely,
if that's your penchant.
Stuff!
That won't lure me.

'Don't try to floor me
with a love potion.
Liquor won't lay me.

'No more malarkey.
Poor williputian,
that will not lure me.
You cannot lay me.'

Psych

Dan   Gill

'You dull moth,
flit. I'm your still
candle flame,
your fixed aim,
the winding path
where you'd stall.'

'Upside down,
that dark reserve
of unlit fire,
your own pyre,
flicker till dawn.
Psych – up yourself.'

Snag

Gill

'Some rose,
briar of barbed wire.
You cannot touch me.
What you clutch,
see, is your hand.
– Take that as read.'

Recorded Message

Dan

'Was love then like anger,
floundering bursts of words,
stark candour we remember?

'Well then, call for anger.
Facefuls can be dished out,
fistfuls, whenever you hanker.

'Anything's better than
the thanks–bearing dead,
this suicide pact to live.'

Dusk to Dawn

Dan   Gill

'This is my good night now.
Let love die, let be.'

'I've found a backwater town.
So stay put, all of a – peace.'

– All darkness through, the sound,
wakings to surf that heaves

over the shingle, flouncing,
you shoulder-haul the sheets.

First light, and the jeering crowd
of breakers that repeat

their Mexican wave up the beach.

Unposted

Dan

There was fire in your eyes
and flame was in your hair,
that bunsen-yellow flare
wavering, parallel to earth.

You heat-riffled the air.
That fly wheel of hips, slow,
off-centred roll, to and fro,
wobbled my whole world . . .

In Living Memory

Dan

No, I have not returned to gloat
in bitter memory,
nor even nostalgic guilt.
It was all too long ago.

I came to read these lichened words
since I'm the very last
of those who knew you, girl,
whose once beloved name
this headstone will casually drop
ever and anon.

It's been some journey,
the light drab.
And now I bid you: drop dead.

II

Sleep Watch

Dan

Hair in a mess.
Such casual sleep,
such nakedness,
all of a heap.

How I would guard
that innocence,
moon-lit and starred,
from all offence.

But you are far
where the dreams hold.
My mere hands are
alien, cold.

Encounter

Dan   *Jo*

'Our mix and match, we're win-tegral,
no dither, caginess, no guile.
How did we, do we, do it, girl?'

> 'Witness squirrels leapt at the news,
> along the branches chased their noise.
> Sparrows flapped – shocked listeners.'

'Then squirrels mark the day, the hour.
So anywhere we find they are
we'll celebrate the day, the year.'

> 'I'd rather they had been the red.
> Then for red letter we could read:
> red squirrel day. The grey's a fraud.'

'Those red beggars are much too rare.
One in a blue moon, they are.
We'd celebrate once an era.'

> 'Red sparrows then. First seen that day
> and we discovered them. They'll do.
> They don't consult the calendar.

> 'They're not endangered, not too local.'
'We'll spot them anywhere we like.
All it'll take's a colluding look.'

Sostenuto

Dan   Jo

'The orchestra concludes.
You are the moment's hush
before applause intrudes
its torrential rush.

'The peal ends over town,
its hum-note in the mind.
All day nothing can drown
that tremor, affined

'to sostenuto silence
everywhere under the din,
like the sense of your presence
under the skin.'

        'Silence? Over my head –
        as in a copper's helmet.
        Anywhere the beat might tread
        Bobby and Nell met.'

Bounce

Dan *Jo*

'When we're in bouncy castle
we're both of us anonymous
and each can be a rascal,
but my, we are contiguous.

'But there's this thing between
that's even more anonymous,
a little imp unseen
– and my, that's both and one of us.

'Names from the family tree
drop windfalls on pseudonymous
– but we shall have to see
if who becomes which monickers.'

Cradle Song

Jo

My precious miniature,
though you're so tiny, cherub,

your little clenching fist,
has clasped my finger fast.

You will not let me go;
I will not let you, girl.

Mine, holding me in sleep,
no dreaming on my lap.

Purr-fect as any cat,
snooze in your cosy cot.

Toast

Dan

So, you are born,
and me no help.
Where have you been,
my little hope?

You birthday parcel,
you're no tomboy.
A pretty puzzle,
I think you'll be.

Your mum, she swears
I've not the faintest
on women's ways.
You'll be a fine test.

So both of us
must learn a bit.
I bet you're boss;
me, butler, butt.

You'll wave your wand,
you mumchance charmer.
I'll be spellbound,
a right performer.

So while you sleep
I'll charm you first:
beach, screlm, glurg, slup.
Sweam dreets, slarp feest.

And welcome home,
you little dream.
Avaunt all harm.
Cheers, with this dram.

Specialist

Dan   *Jo*

'You must become
a specialist in mud.
It helps with all the crud
about her bum
and will be knowledge
useful to employ
– with any boy pre-college.'

Evening Lullaby

Jo

Snuffly one,
the milk's all gone,
and so's the sun;
the moon's still wan
in the lingering light.

Little one,
glide like the swan,
now day is done,
on the moon-shone
lake of the night.

Chubby one,
sleep, drifting on
slow dreams homespun.
Hubbub begone.
Sleep, little mite.

Greedy one,
my sleep soon gone,
you jump the sun,
my tachyon,
small diner-mite.

Guzzly one,
the milk's all gone,
and here's the sun;
the moon's outshone
in the rising light.

Sprint

Jo

Because my mind is curled round joy
I run and run in this summer rain,
a girl, a girl, and next a boy.
Yards, yards before I feel a drop.
So cool this rain. I cannot stop.

Signs and Wonders

Jo

Milking time, here comes your moo.
This is me and that's your feed.

Sign-language, me, teach it you?
You are all the signs I need.

Everything you show is true.
All your gestures I can heed.

Sleepy smile, is that a clue?
Happiness is what I read.

Being

Jo

You dainty little thing,
how can you ever bear
the weight of this heavy love? –

Oh, in this late, late spring –
like the bumbly bee-brer,
clumping in a foxglove.

They said they didn't sting
when, small, I used to scare,
dreading the way they'd shove:

in its mouth rummaging.
It didn't seem very fair.
I was afraid – am.

Meditation

Jo

One bloom, this. The times, years, I tell myself
I shall remember one, this season to next,
when roses sway, heavy as my bare breasts . . .
Now that these blooms again confuse the sense
what comes into the mind is love, as I bend
over the briars and cut the faded heads.
The blazon everywhere of unaccountable fire,
unretellable by the symmetricating mind.

The Last Nursery Rhyme

Jo

Close your ears,
sleepy head.
We're tucking you up
in your last bed
with these tears
and this dreadful story
that if you wake
you will remember
the hands that snugged you here
and we won't be far away.
You little pretender,
lie doggo. I'll play.

III

Aside

Dan

Gone. You're gone.
And with you
dies a boy.

And a man
dies also.
– Hush, fool, hush.

So sudden
your leaving;
slow this, slow.

Mother and
child should grow
responsive.

Too quick, you,
inveigling
her, life-long.

Dear fastness,
you keep her,
frail, changeless.

Find a way
to leave go,
poor changeling.

Monody

Dan   Jo

So small your mouth was,
so long your cries last.
Mine must be silent.

No sorrow outwards.
Her face such grieving,
mine shall be secret.

A thing once spokcn
cannot be silenced –
circles in cipher.

It must not open.
The wound is clean now.
The body will heal it.

Gently caressing,
lover to lover,
we'll make some comfort.

Love is the presence
nothing can smother.
– Give us a cuddle.

Millstream

Dan   *Jo*

'Here we are. Look:
that rake-head of light,
its silver tines across the weir.

'Downstream of the bridge,
cloisonné eddy ripples . . .

'It will do
for now.'

A river ran through childhood
with bathing, rafts, dams, yachts –
lost model launch.

Marked wreck . . . The broadening water's
wicker weave of shadow
through the light.

Dog

Dan

Dog, I remember you. Much else,
and, maybe more important, forget,
some for good reason, some for less,
people or things, whatever, gone.

Carrying that fathom of branch,
balanced in your jaws, between
the lake's edge and striding boots.
A tightrope walker with his pole,
you swayed with never a wet paw.
No one was playing fetch with you.
You chose it for yourself. Two yards.

Stop hounding me dog. Just go,
keeping from water a fathom of grief.

Night-Watch

Jo

We live in each other's hands,
untentative.

But never sleep facing each other
where the dreams weep.

Is it you, little one,
sleeping where you shouldn't,
between the two of us?

Playtime

Jo

Arms out stiff
like boards to gather leaves,
yellow ribbon fluttering.

Quick, child, quick.
But you will not catch the robin,
no, nor that sparrow.

We used to call them spadgers
when little like you.
But I can't stay here

and watch you playing
as my daughter . . .
Just a year dead.

And there's nowhere else.

Track

Dan   *Jo*

'It marks a beaten path, years overgrown,
between two ancient settlements long gone.

'Before a way was worn into the earth,
who knew if haven waited on its path?'

'Or, if the way were trodden from beyond,
who knew some settlement would be this end?

'How come a walker knew what was to give
or take at either end – if not a grave?'

'The trudge of outcasts year on year? Or road
trodden by generations of the crowd?

'Pilgrims to some wood-henge of bloodied earth?
Vestiges, but not the scorch-mark of a hearth.

'Our hands reach out and join up like a path.
We'll keep the traces open.'

Memento

Dan

Not as this loss, but as a little person,
how shall I remember you? You had no words
except coo, gurgle, yell; you had no life
except the milk, the smiles, your tiny fists,
loud lady, that you clenched or clasped a world
of fingers with, and then you let us go.

– And left these photographs, your smiles, your sleep,
your bath, a little gloss on stinky you.
And most in clothes of nameless whites or pinks.
Look, here's an ancient photo of your gran.
You never saw her nor she you. Your photographs –
I'll pick you up – look at each other now.

I do remember where that shot was snapped,
in days of sepia, black, whites and greys.
See, it was 'poshly' tinted afterwards.
The colours for the sea-wall and the beach,
the sky and houses seem more or less right.
You might say it was verisimilitude.

– That's a long word between the two of us.
And yet these colours for her clothes, her bag,
I can't recall as hers. They're gone from mind.
I was her ten-year-old and then she died,
oh, far too soon she went and left us boys.
That grin I say I know . . . but maybe not.

Perhaps her odd expression as she tries
to tie her headscarf in a rising wind.
The only picture of her that we have.
– All these: you sleeping peacefully, you smily.
Charmer, oh, this is all you'll ever be.
These cannot change as other children's will.

Bourn

(Dan) Gill

Patience, it can't all be gone.
No. We'd be back there again:

the chestnut spires be fresh and clean –
the bourn's fordable down the lane.

Yes. We'll make it there again,
alone, in dream, where we began.

Hands across that rustic divide,
what a day that was: we vowed

each other a life. This void,
these feuilletons reviewed and reviewed.

Sparrows

Jo

Matt grey sky,
the still air,
dark stream – dull sparrow backs,
legging it downhill.

– Spadgers once,
in a puddle of sun,
your song a hop and flit –
uncatchable.

My shadow,
playing you tag,
splashing down.
Wings away . . .

– Come on,
sunshine, sparkle up
my missed sparrow.
Not these shudders.

Album

Dan   *Jo*

'It never does you any good.
Don't look at those. Please give it me.
Let's find repeatable scenes. Look,
this one, summer, tracking that stream:

'tumbledown lock-gate by the path.
I posed you there, half turned. Or these –'
                    'Oh, definitely, Meadow Farm,
                    but that's not the highlight for me,

                    'walking the stream back to its source
                    at a ragged angle to all this.
                    That's not what I was going for,
                    the boggy bit you called a spring.

                    'No, what I focus still's a flower,
                    soapwort, a garden fugitive.
                    Let's find that in the album now,
                    and both of us looking for it.'

IV

Concert

Dan

The Brahms Cello Concerto, opus 102:
that horn-player, your figure, your face,
spit image from the mind's eye, you,
not a day older.
                 – Another life you never had
and never could have had; like all of those
we missed by fate or grace.
And now this Brahms becomes your music,
another chimera settling into the mind's truth.

Attrition

Dan   (Gill)

If it would do any good,
if it would stir any feeling,
even for the erosion of years,
I would telepath how many nights
you enter my dreams at a tangent –
you who
          disremember dream.

Nativity Play

Dan

To this silt plain you've followed me,
where no hills echo human voice
or any lively thing
and these piles of books are most use
for reefing curtains bulged with wind,
implacable from the east.

Homesick, you start to deck the room
early for a merry Christmas,
though none of our friends,
willing or not, could make the distance.
Poor, stunted, unplastic tree.
No lights. – Some shelter for you.

You spiral crepe streamers on the pelmet,
stick tape, wobble to fix them up,
teetering for help.
The tape won't hold long on this stuff.
I take up my book again.
The curtains swell, one streamer down.

You kick the books closer to the hems,
furiously drag the steps back.
We fix it. Till when?
You soldier on. I pick up the book,
not really reading, await the descent
and your head cradled in my arms.

New Year

Dan   *Jo*

'This we have sworn:
"Whither thou goest I will go."
– Where we go the memories track.
The child is born.'
'This is the only way I know.'
'You gave your word. Let us go back.'

'Mud does not yearn.'
'The broken hope is not the land's.
The hills were not our enemies.
Let us return.
High earth sinks to estuary sands.
Not seasonal, the memories.

'It's time to pack.
I need the sheltered nooks, tree-cover.
My mind is nothing here, not here.
I shall go back.
I cannot bear this level wuther.
Let us return to the old new year.'

Dawn Chorus

Dan   *(Jo)*

– Birds . . . Even you scratchy birds,
protected bats in my belfry,
more troublesome than words . . .
                inside a copper's helmet.

                – Spadgers,
ubiquitous sparrows,
squabbling like grubby urchins.
Killers with your beaky arrows,
you target her. Slow murder.

She's given you her secret name.
That is your power over her.
Nowhere on earth beyond your aim.
You target her. Cold murder.

No chance of your extinction.
No habitable place on earth
where I could take her, not an inch
you cannot touch in her.

Dog Days

Dan   *Jo*

'Russet ears down,
head on parallel paws,
dozing in the sun.' –
                'Haunches wide for coolness
                like his wing armchair.'

'Doggo, red setter.'

Disjunction

Dan   (Gill)

An avenue of overhanging boughs.
Two boys,
        their knees like scrubbed carrots,
chase each other in the flick of shadows
where iridescent fish-scales of sunlight
catch the corner of the eye.

They do not see the avenue. It's trunks.
Nor the perspective dropping away.
They dodge about and tack towards the by-pass
where the bus like a red-admiral
flitters briefly and out of sight.

Sweltered under glass of a long journey,
travelling straight through this near convergence,
I glimpse an avenue of birch and pine
and two boys who do not see a man
on the bus I hope they'll always miss.

Ah, momentary boys without a name,
unnoticed trees, unmetalled track,
gone now, long gone, except for half a name:
Glotters Road – no more apostrophe –
and this bus I hope they always missed.

V

Afterthought

Dan   (Gill)

Sometimes even an apple can do it,
that chomp in your speech.
– If I could admit and bring to mind the friends
I thought I'd not much miss but do
and that poor memory could reach
to make a few recall old friends
they'd like to find,
would you catch the half smile we had
as we turned aside and you as usual said:
        'See you soon. Ciao.'
– It's a long while
since that lost day we never knew was last,
without much notice, went on into the night.
Do either of us mind it now?

Valerian

Dan   *Jo*

'I've given up my time to flowers
and I shall put some on your grave.
You'll have as much clue then as now.
White valerian, that's what I say.
Why argue? Never mind the ruin.
White valerian, it was, today.'

'This time, valerian, white
if you insist. And next time
we'll settle on a Norman site.
This almost-togetherness. How
we have managed to live with it,
year in, year out. It won't change now.'

'White valerian, none too rare,
famous for clinging to any old wall.'

I take it there's a red elsewhere.

Telepathetic

Dan   (Gill)

Each other's lives held in our hands. –
     'Oh love, live longer than the robin.'
Remember.
Not to slip through the fingers like sinking sands.
Poor little ember.

And here I go again today.
I cannot help myself. I wish I could.
Where are you? Which of us lost the way?
Was it ever much good?

Still sense the moment if I think
of you? – Reticulations of the net
of shadow on the river stretch and shrink,
retaining the light fret.

Breeze-scuffed water, matt like dark moss,
under the canopy of trees. The eye
a camera, the memory a chaos
and probably both a lie.

    Poor fool robin, that fights itself
    matched in a bit of mirror on the bank. –
I will not think you're dead. How could I tell
where that blank butts on this?

If thought can emanate from the fit
that makes it, I charge the air, I charge you: think
of me. – Oh, any river does for it.
Where nets of shadow link.

That bourn, even. Think as you taste:
memory that will freeze Lethe slick,
and skitter across intact – my ice-blade
temper of thought. Dead quick.

Music

Dan   Jo

'Swan neck, bare arm
of the woman violinist,
dipping to the music,
beak shaking –'

        'Swan as in those summers
        we thought we had
        and remember like this . . .

        'And that dirndl skirt –'
'swaying
a circle of fanned-out pigeon-tails.'

Cameo

(Dan) Gill

A young girl in sling-backs
scurries along the river walk
in the lank shadows of sunset
towards the bridge and bus-stop,
cutting a dash, her evening out.

On a far hill an old woman
looks down on the dry valley,
watching a girl dawdle the path,
tallied off by willows, a river's
liquorice ribbon skimmed with glints.

The cod-flakes of cloud parting.
Did she see them? A bird's cry,
the yard broom scraped over concrete.
How many broom-birds? –
Miss Flashing
hasn't heard a thing. That heron. –

She shows a leg to board the bus
whose destination seemed a number. –
Sleeping a catch off, fixed as a post,
sunning – or could it be a chink
of silver birch through curtains of willow?

Trio

Dan   Gill   Jo

You thought you'd know her – by your dying day.
How green her eyes, so dark her voice and low.
You won't admit the memories that stay.

Do those years count? You'd thought there was a way.
You had such friends and plans. Your watch was slow.
You thought you'd know her till your dying day.

      The windows you looked out of – kids at play.
      The blossom on the cherry. Was it snow?
      You cannot hug the memories that stay.

Who keeps a record of what is to pay.
The zeroes mount, and no line's drawn below.
And to your credit just a dying day.

      No glass can mirror absence turning grey.
      And what you see is nothing much to show.
      You do not choose the memories that stay.

Whatever you betrayed time will betray.
      The fonts outlast the names that we bestow.
You thought you'd know her till your dying day.
You do not want the memories to stay.

Footbridge

Dan   *Jo*

'Look, now we have turned, do you see how
vee-frames of the bridge cast their shadow
echoingly faint on the far side's
wire-lattice, but skewed by the angle?

'How often we've taken our walk here
nor seen in the odd burst of sunshine
that delicate cross-hatch of shading.
Now when there's a chance we will spot it.'

– One day here our last walk together.
Then, oh, then may nothing noteworthy
way-mark any point in the mind's eye.
Like most of the rest strolled as usual. –

'"Thundering Swan Duckboard". Remember?
Two swans had just skimmed us in take off;
both ducked the near miss of their wing-claps.
We'll call today "Shadow Bridge Saunter".'

The Bay

Dan   (Gill)

It was a day all sun.
Two great speedboat bow-waves,
your hair swathed back as you run
towards me laughing and you say:

    Wow, what a glorious bay.
    Where better could you have now?
– You burst out in the old way
but not, I suppose, with a will.

The bay swishes its ebbing frill,
recedes with its soft soughing,
dwindles to this pale blue . . .
    squill.
What a thing to hold you now.

– Sorry, old yen, it's
    ciao.
Your image haunts another eye,
ghosts for my daughter, your age now
she'd be. Another goodbye.

Summertime

Dan   *Jo*

        'Always such tall storeys, the hollyhocks.
        Beginning to open. Look.'
'And the furled buds
always recall those paper twists of salt
in crisps we had post-war to celebrate
festivities of some sort.'
        'Blue? The full blooms
        remind me of those loudspeaker horns
        four to a pole at summer fetes or dos.'
'Grey? – Odd how the occasions slip away.'
        'Not my mother's country saying, overheard
        at play, too often later: When the top flower
        on the hollyhocks is done summer is over.'
'Ah, we both remember the salt, the twist.'
        Tears – annuals
– wintergral.

VI

Sleight

Gill

They spin not, neither do they reap. –
Across the corner of the eye,
they spin, or so it seems to me,
angle of vision, angle of flight.

Kids' paper windmills come to mind,
that spun or fluttered in the breeze.
These spinners, sparrows and their like.
– But the wind rose. The noise increased:

starlings scrambling, the vanes whirred,
flapping on sticks.
                         Yet why should that
bring back a bourn, dry half the year,
the ford that summer a water splash,
and the illusion that you were?
And this illusion that I am?

Late, Late Autumnal

Jo

'I went striding out, not, as in summer,
we seem to mosey round the hillsides:
old-gold, fire-orange and raw umbers,
less blatant than the dog-days' brilliance.

'They called to mind those childish crayons –
scrub-scrub for sky, no cloudless azure;
a yellow spider for the sun blazing,
that greened the blue in taunting fashion.

'A child's pictogram of a bird flying,
two hedges swept up from the centre.
So, to the bird's eye of the cipher
I strode, in hopes of stile, not fences.'

... There was the stile and, sitting pretty,
a young girl watched my progress, frowning,
the auburn of her hair befitted
the turning colours of the rowan.

– I stared you back to fix my smile,
some likeness, on your looks. Not a glimmer.
And yet I'll call you daughter. Child,
child, how we make things in our image.

Déjà Vu

Jo

In another season
that flashed across us like a jay
among these same beeches
we wept for joy.

This bitter wind makes tears
I don't know if I want them real.

Mist

(Dan) Gill

Soft, blurring wisps drifting in.
Whopping powder-puffs of mist
snag then fray on the hanger broccoli;
knee-level mousse across the mead.
The haze of first love.

This downy white inner plush,
these broad-bean pods.
Fist
love, velvet reminders embrangle
over and under all.

Over all –
all-perviant.
Overall,
the old-green nubbled shuck.

Not Sent

Jo

You're off to college maybe now,
your ties with home grown tenuous.
There had to come the time for this.
You, strike out for the nothing new.

So mum will fire long letters off,
fussing about your ways and welfare
and you will turn the teenage waffler
and never let her feel you're safe.

There's nothing to write home about,
that's what you'll think, or even say.
And she'll write weather or vacancy,
angling for something you might bite.

There you'd still sit upon your fence
or stile, frowning at her approach,
bothered she'll lecture you or preach,
when what you need's a large advance.

Well, here's her first unanswered letter,
ghost-written by a passing whim,
not vacancy but vacuum,
the first instalment of dead litter.

Threnody

(Dan) Gill

The hands repulsed,
my sea–salt dead.
The nights convulsed
in my narrow bed.

Not what I miss
but think I missed
milling out this
tread–sugar grist.

The touchless men
in wakeful dream,
not now and then
but semen to seem.

Such phalluses
once upended.
These galaxies
nightly befriended.

Flicker till dawn,
psych yourself
    – down.
    Just watch stars spawn,
backwater town.

Heath

Dan   *Jo*

'Some climb.
Those silver birch,
their runnels of dirty snow
delta back to the sky.'
'There, look: dry leaves, gust-blown,
sparrow across brown earth.'

'Why birch
and not the pine
that needs the silver bark,
though sharing the same rise?
Why anti-camouflage?
Most living things will hide.'

The dark pane of sky splits,
broken by lightning cracks.
You're cowering in my arms.
This is our habitat,
and our hugs stand out in it

like silver birch,
caresses
that, sure as we cling hold,
won't make the lightning shift.
Yet my hands console you –
console me in your quiescence.

And love, we hope,
is not deceit,
and we have lived by this
collusion.
And the gusts of dead leaves
don't sparrow off.

Indelible

Dun   (Gill)

Turning slowly at the field's edge
that birch and now me with it,
one branch the line of your gesture,
as though you held a glass of wine
toward the light.

You tried to turn my head that day.
Times out of mind,
remote, malign, you hold out still.
It's all my eye.
You weren't mine, not by a long sight.

That was your game, to take the eye
            – Eastern delicacy dipped in brine.
Still, now, I see through it
a hazy sun
burring the line of a birch with light.

Harbour View

Dan   Jo

Coiling long plaits,
dangling a sandal,
skew on the sea-wall.

So many glimpses,
so many visions.
These ungathered pasts.

The Wild Buccaneer

Gill (singing)

Robin, your breast is much too red,
dodging among the clods.
How recklessly you bob your head
where the fork prods.

Oh robin, why so red a breast?
The earth you peck is brown,
the leaves are green, now blue the west
where ships dip down.

Cock robin, chip of chirpy song,
bean-flowers, like butterflies
in scatty flight, are blown along
above your eyes.

Some say the wind blows where it listeth
and no one knows its coming.
It chills the body of this death,
deafening, dumbing.

Whose are these soul sighs in the wind?
His voice I cannot quell.
Where must it wander, gale-force dinned
over the swell?

Imploring wind that backs and veers,
you take these words of mine
and whish them into noisy ears,
come rain or shine:

'O love, live longer than the robin
that fights its own reflection,
matched in a shard of mirror, bobbing
its blood complexion.'

Oh robin, robin, fading coal
in embers of the year,
blow in next spring, red banderole,
wild buccaneer.

VII

Oriel

Dan

The seasons are all wrong these days.
Silhouetted in the unweeping willow
a few late migrant birds,
semiquavers.
The last dead leaves on sharper view.

A ghost flits in the oriel opposite,
into light, then back from the window.
The silver birch, gust swayed,
puppet-masters
the to and froing wraith of the sill.

Half turned you muse over the gardens
part of a picture not where you are.
Skies, sheaves – burrs in your hair?
Past laughter
a sycamore seed-wing at the corner of your eye.

Night-Piece

Jo

We look over the gardens
toward the far fields
in the stillness of twilight,

as if, in the war, kids trying
to stretch the light out
into the edge of darkness,

giving our lank shadows the slip
in shadow trees bridging
the river to our side,

in those long days of sunlight
our parents cussed as
double the summer time,

wrapped in our own outcry,
hiding from the name-shouts
calling the night in.

Lead

Dan

The soldiers have long been broken or lost,
a grudged relief when patched-up ones went missing:
those matchstick-mounted heads, plasticine arms.
– And that trilbied farmer,
feet bent off by his tractor,
who got the toothpick stilts.
All of them mourned in their time.

Yet, in the lost child's eye,
that glisten of the hidden lead,
the inner gleam of a loved thing,
never again so lighted on.

Slippage

Dan   *Jo*

'Just bits. Yes, both of them –
the long-stemmed glasses,
our favourites.
One I might have caught
in mid-air fumbling.'

– Tense for the smash of splintered light,
but the helplessness
spreading anywhere.

> Inch by inch and all.
> No end of watching. ·
> We are in free fall
> and flinching up for the crash.

Roses

Gill

Idiot roses
that try it on again each year
with all this bloody colour,

I know you
like the back of my hand
that reaches out
to pick you, shaking,

where worm veins surface,
expecting rain,
but these dry bones
will not live again.

Stroll

Dan   *Jo*

'This chill air's like apples just not sharp.'
'Despite myself I like it: mists that wear
away that world's end shelf out of the scarp.'
'The trees are smoking off to powdered air.'
'And this near silence nearly deceives the ear.'
'Look, that squirrel vanishing, its tail
a plume of frosted breath.'
'Now can you hear
the lackadaisical drops that tock the trail?

'Mist in your hair, cold at my fingertips
and my misgivings give against the grain:
solidity spirited off!'
'And half our steps
in this dark mould of leaves and times outgrown
are tracked by doubt to key into the mind
this peace, this beauty . . . '
'as if it might be meant.'

Voices in the Head

Dan   Gill   Jo

If time reversed, or frayed
until the self were freed,

    we shall meet, ghost to ghost,
    vacuous, outraged, aghast,

    as in rough justice we should,
    the mind's attritus be shared,

what more is left to say
to aural vacancy?

        – Have a look-say? Fat chance.
        Wavers of scéantific chintz,

        sound-bites guessing the fare
        across the inanosphere.

        She's happy where she is?
        Medium happiness?

        Oh, make it up? Fine speeches,
        ironies, purple patches:

We'd world enough and time;
no hindsight can redeem.

        'The stars are my silent cry ... '?
        They're hot at mimicry,

pinpricks of pique in the night,
the pointilliste infinite.

Look, the shadow of clouds
the gathering dark occludes.

You asked me to come through walls
with my
infrangible waltz.

In fourteen days, you said.
Sorry. Delays my side.

Oh, you franged my wall
all right. Kept my word well.

Memory circles, moth,
spiralling, burnt to a myth;

no deus-ex hard-wired,
random access, chance word;

no leads out of the labyrinth
holding the ghost of a wraith.

Duet

Dan   *Jo*

'What shall we make these days
the moments of vision of?'
                'Something a half-seen creature does,
                or nuance of light above?'

'The startling light in a known eye
at a strange turn of the day' –
                'Some insight widdershins as bryony,
                the verve of a wild idea?'

'Dearest, let's look on each other
with gleams of an old surprise.' –
                'As when our first swifts came over
                and compelled us into praise?'

'Though we know now they were' –
                'all of our visionaries, wrong' –
'and no longer want the fancy ware
they pushed when they were young,

'let us lie with each other
complicitly, old feisty love.'
                'Each of us speak peace in either,
                and a little more live.'

Blowing Bubbles

Dan   (Gill)   (Jo)

The bubble speech balloon in my brain
'said' to the
           spherical inane:

'Vague child, all grandparents, so it's said,
enjoy you grandlings since the selfish gene
rejoices in the length of years ahead.
Let's call this theory the evolutionary mean.

'And other jokers call it our joint attack
with you against the common enemy.
Grandparents share your fun and let the flak
land parents with your tantrums – demony-denimy.

'Black-humorists will swear we're just indulgent
of you because we want to live again
our childhood days and see our youth refulgent.
– That's black enough, a fulgurating pain.

'Well. You'll decide nearer my age, tick-tock.
You kids are divertimenti, play us an encore
as you run up the hickory-dickory dock
and we run down it
           willy-nilly-wonkier.

'Avaunt all harm. Cheers. Long may your onspring
be just as lively as my offspring's wanting.'

VIII

Skyscape

(Dan) Gill

The skies I've daydreamed at: seen fells
and firths,
backwaters,
lakes, moors.
Most I forget but I won't this:
pale pink and blue stripes, parallel
and horizontal, with that dip
of awnings shading summer lawns . . .

Who else was under that awning? Why
remember? What were we playing at,
old flames my head still flickers with?
– That old clout caught on the barbed wire,
a pigeon once, fluffed by the wind.
But why remember bird – or rag? . . .

If any of you are soldiering on –
or sailoring – and catch this sky,
do you see through? What should we see?
Whose memory leaves something lost
and longed for there? Or, wiped clean,
come niggling back into the mind?

Bright then, not bleached by too much light –
the unbreachable canopy . . . Night-night.

Gust

Jo

Silver birch.
Bits of it blow off
and turn into two magpies.
Old joy.

Reprise

Dan   *Jo*

    'Do not say pardon if you do not hear.
    The time is past when there's much new to say.
    No need to answer, guessing something near.

    'The living words we spoke by heart and ear,
    who prompted whom?'
'Impromptu was the play.'
    'Do not say pardon if you do not hear.

    'Our word we gave each other, firm and clear.' –
'The sotto voce of our day-to-day.' –
    'No need to answer, guessing something near.

    'The waterfalling words.'
'The white, combed weir.'
    'The countless swans'
'we counted'
    'flown away.

Do not say pardon if you do not hear.

'Sound waves ring out for ever and a year,
beyond the hearing in acoustic spray.
No need to answer.'
'Dearest, oh, my dear.'

'Silence is second nature, the inner ear.
No need for radio telescope's array.
Do not ask pardon: nothing is so clear.
I won't repeat myself. I won't be here.'

Soliloquy

Dan

I used to say:
'You go to sleep now,'
and you would.

You knew it would take
hours for me
to catch you up.

And I'm still here,
you poor old thing,
still awake,

talking in your sleep,
trying not to say,
not to wake you:

'Sleep, my dearest,
stay asleep.'
– Whispers as if

tomorrow we'll both
be here
in our old love.

Graveside

Dan

The earth lies over you.
My nights are turned to days
and I cannot sleep.
Such a little darkness
and all this light.

Rear-View Mirror

Dan   *(Jo)*

They laid out the way
as we looked ahead
but no one said
it would be this way.

It was not our way
when we looked back
but a . . .
                beaten track
                and the only way.

– My poor red sparrows.

Twitch

Dan   *(Jo)*

Look, I would say if you were here –
if you were still here, I should say:
We once . . .
We never saw a goldfinch together, did we?
And today I see two.
The last time I saw one was as a kid,
the first was in a book. I learnt to draw it.
And today I see two.
Whoosh, straight in that tree.
How do they take off sideways from chain-link?
Why do they like that . . .
                tree of heaven,
isn't that its silly name? You would have told me.
Not yellow, gold. Oh, it was gold.